THE LAND BALLOT

D0280483

Fleur Adcock was born in New Zealand in 1934. She spent the war years in England, returning with her family to New Zealand in 1947. She emigrated to Britain in 1963, working as a librarian in London until 1979. In 1977-78 she was writer-in-residence at Charlotte Mason College of Education, Ambleside. She was Northern Arts Literary Fellow in 1979-81, living in Newcastle, becoming a freelance writer after her return to London. She received an OBE in 1996, and the Queen's Gold Medal for Poetry in 2006 for *Poems 1960-2000* (Bloodaxe Books, 2000).

Fleur Adcock published three pamphlets with Bloodaxe: *Below Loughrigg* (1979), *Hotspur* (1986) and *Meeting the Comet* (1988), as well as her translations of medieval Latin lyrics, *The Virgin & the Nightingale* (1983). All her other collections were published by Oxford University Press until they shut down their poetry list in 1999, after which Bloodaxe published her collected poems, *Poems 1960-2000* (2000), followed ten years later by *Dragon Talk* (2010); then by *Glass Wings* (2013) and *The Land Ballot* (2015).

FLEUR ADCOCK

The Land Ballot

BLOODAXE BOOKS

Copyright © Fleur Adcock 2015

ISBN: 978 1 78037 147 4

First published 2015 by
Bloodaxe Books Ltd,
Eastburn,
South Park,
Hexham,
Northumberland NE46 1BS

and by Victoria University Press
in New Zealand.

www.bloodaxebooks.com
For further information about Bloodaxe titles
please visit our website or write to
the above address for a catalogue.

Supported using public funding by
**ARTS COUNCIL
ENGLAND**

LEGAL NOTICE

All rights reserved. No part of this book may be
reproduced, stored in a retrieval system, or
transmitted in any form, or by any means, electronic,
mechanical, photocopying, recording or otherwise,
without prior written permission from Bloodaxe Books Ltd.

Requests to publish work from this book
must be sent to Bloodaxe Books Ltd.

Fleur Adcock has asserted her right under
Section 77 of the Copyright, Designs and Patents Act 1988
to be identified as the author of this work.

Cover design: Neil Astley & Pamela Robertson-Pearce.

Printed in Great Britain by Bell & Bain Limited, Glasgow, Scotland, on
acid-free paper sourced from mills with FSC chain of custody certification.

i.m. Cyril John Adcock, 1904-1987

and

Samuel Adcock, 1876-1956

Evangeline Adelaide Mary Adcock, née Eggington (Eva), 1875-1970

ACKNOWLEDGEMENTS

I should like to thank the Alexander Turnbull Library and the NZ National Library for research materials, Catherine Jehly of the Te Awamutu Museum for her patience in supplying me with numerous extracts from the *Waipa Post*, and the staff of the Pirongia Heritage and Information Centre for their advice and their enthusiastic response to this project when I visited the centre in April 2013.

I am also grateful to the following publications in which some of these poems have appeared: *Australian Book Review, PN Review, The Arts of Peace: an Anthology*, ed. Adrian Blamires and Peter Robinson (Two Rivers Press and the English Association, 2014), *The Rialto, The Spectator*, and *Wellington Festival Anthology 2004*.

CONTENTS

Life is real! Life is earnest!
And the grave is not its goal;
Dust thou art, to dust returnest,
Was not spoken of the soul.

HENRY WADSWORTH LONGFELLOW

Life is butter.
Life is but a
melon cauliflower,
melancholy flower.
Life is butter melon,
life is butter melon
cauliflower,
cauliflower.

CAMPFIRE SONG

We had some very happy times at Te Rau-a-moa and were
very fond of our 'Squirrel'

CONDOLENCE CARD FROM DOSSIE
(DOROTHEA) McMONAGLE, NÉE DASSLER.

Where the Farm Was

He is not there/ I am not there,
but we are haunting it somewhat,
gliding a few feet above the ground
in perhaps detectably thin air.

I am half-occupying the eyes
of my young father, still in his teens –
much of which he spent, like his school-mates,
in bare feet on the back of a horse.

Therefore as we scan the horizon
two equine ears (which he doesn't notice,
being used to them) swing up and down
at the lower frame of our field of vision.

Probably he's keeping a lookout
even now for those confounded cattle,
five of them, that strayed into the bush
as in a nursery rhyme. Our conjoined sight

is in his keeping. When I gained access
by wriggling into his optic nerves
it was as a hitchhiker, merely;
he controls direction and focus.

In return I get the benefit
of his 20/20. Distant green froth
resolves into identifiable
trees, with specific leaves. Any minute

beyond the newly brought-in land
(fields, would he still say, or paddocks?)
flickers of movement will solidify
into the birds he never mentioned.

The Sower

In the beginning was the axe, then fire.
The first instalment happened before they came:
his father had arranged for Mr Daysh
to fell fourteen acres of standing timber,
lop off and burn the smaller branches,
and leave an area ready to be sown.

Sam was working dawn to dusk on the house,
but sowing was a job a boy could do.

Into the velvety ash, once it had cooled,
he walked like an image from the New Testament
broadcasting seed from a sack at his waist
in swathes and arcs and parabolas
to bring forth a fresh green beard:
the potash would turn it into a meadow.

That was the second power he harnessed.
The first was his first horse: ha ha!

(You've seen the photograph: a lad of eleven
in knickerbockers, reins in his hand,
posing aloft for the glass negative;
although this was earlier, at Te Rahu –
some special occasion, else why would his father
be standing beside him in a three-piece suit?)

But what do I know? Only what he told us,
and what Sam wrote in that pocket diary.

The Pioneer

The way the land ballot worked was like this:
if your name came up you might be offered
the block you'd applied for or another,
which you had to take, or you got nothing.
Meanwhile you looked for something else to do.

Sam was a master packing-case maker,
but New Zealand made no packing-cases.
His other mastery was hairdressing;
he found a job in Te Awamutu
with a barber called Dwen, and they waited,

renting the teacher's house at Te Rahu
three miles away, befriending the farmer
next door, learning to milk, and waiting, while
ballot after ballot came up null, and
waiting, and buying a horse, and waiting.

When they heard, he rushed hot-foot to see it:
his hundred and fifty acres of bush
at Te Rauamoa, halfway along
the road (if road it deserved to be called)
from Otorohanga to Kawhia.

As if to meet a new mail-order bride
he strode off, perhaps quaking a little
(things turn folkloric if you wait too long).
He went by train to Otorohanga
and then walked – it may have been twenty miles.

At one point he had to cross a river;
unable to swim, he waded through it.
One mile road frontage of native forest,
to be transformed somehow into pasture,
waiting on that mountainside. Up he trudged.

Sam's Diary

I

For 1914, but with an afterlife:
blue cloth binding, falling apart,
the *Order of the Sons of Temperance
Friendly Society* badge on the cover,

the back pages overflowing with
a 40-year palimpsest of addresses,
and those at the front with payments, notes, accounts,
and cryptic visitations from the future.

In the centre months a sprinkle of entries
for 1914 itself, chatty at first:
*June 20: Set sail 2.15,
passed the Welsh coast and Isle of Anglesey*

*where Pilot left us at 7 o'clock;
found two stowaways. Retired 9.30.
June 21: felt bad all day*
[and so on through the Bay of Biscay];

*children very costive, gave castor oil.
June 23: got up feeling better.*
After which life rolled on unrecorded:
Cyril pushing his baby cousin's pram

up and down the deck (not that Sam tells us),
Eva doing whatever she quietly did,
ports flitting by – Las Palmas, Durban –
names only. No mention of the storm

in the Indian Ocean, against which
hatches were battened down and oil poured
literally on the waves – one metaphor
after another brought to life – in vain.

Then on August 8, four days after
the official declaration was made,
News of the war,
followed by silence.

II

Scantling
Rough lining
Clean weather board
Dressed timber flooring

Scantling
Weather bd
Dressed timber
Sills
F boards –

pencil notes ghosting the pages
intended for January 1914.
Then a flutter of dates blown in from elsewhere,
with just enough details to anchor them :

Came to Te Rau Moa Wed May 17
Mr Daysh helped Thurs May 18 – 6 hrs
Frid May 19 – 6 hrs
[and so on to Wed May 24].

These fit the calendar for 1916 –
where suddenly, it seems, we've arrived
all hands helping to clear the site,
burn off debris and build the house:

the Daysh boys and their father employed
by the hour for such time as they could spare;
the hired carpenter, Bebbington,
for seventeen days running into June;

Sam, himself no mean joiner, sawing up
scantling for joists and keeping accounts:

Oilcloth 10 yds 2s 3d   *£1.2.6*
       5 yds 2/-   *10.6*
3 ft stretcher & mattress   *17.3*
Enamel   *2.6*
Oats & bag   *7.3*
Bicycle   *£3*

And a bucolic note: *Cow served*
November 21st 1915;
due August 1916. Not long
to wait; she was pregnant when they bought her.

DISTRICT NEWS: TE RAU-A-MOA

(Own Correspondent)

A number of new houses have lately been erected here, all the bricks for the chimneys being burned at the local kiln. Mr Bebbington is erecting a commodious residence for Mr Murrell. All the timber has been cut and the joinery made locally.

The timber is already on the ground for Mr Adcock's new house on Pirongia West junction, the owner intending to reside on his farm at an early date. It will be remembered that Mr Adcock's land was acquired only a few months ago from the Crown, it being a locked reserve for nearly twenty years.

The district has other locked lands – about 5,000 acres – partly bush and partly fern. Blackberries have lately been spreading over these lands at a rapid rate, and it is hoped the Crown Lands Department will take steps to clear these weeds or else throw the block open for selection.

The Okoko Valley, where the blackberries grow most abundantly, has for several years been a favourite blackberry-ing spot for the settlers for miles around. This valley, which is richly carpeted with native grass and partly grown over with native bush, is an ideal picnic ground, and has been used as such for the last fifteen years. It is a pity a few acres were not cut out as a picnic ground for all time.

Waipa Post, 31 March 1916

Bedtime Story

But there are no tigers in this forest
to run round and round a tree until they

turn into butter; this is not jungle
but unbroached New Zealand bush, and it is

the trees themselves – rimu, hinau, tawa,
totara – that because they cannot run

will be turned step by step first into ash
then grass, then milk, then, yes, into butter.

I trust no one has any objections?
(Hang around as the century scrolls by).

The Fencer   *(Cyril speaks)*

'Fencing to begin with was a pragmatic
zigzaggy affair, taking advantage
of the logs lying pell–mell everywhere –

you couldn't walk a dozen steps for logs –
and rolling or stacking smaller stuff to bridge
the gaps between one huge felled trunk and the next.

Once the first grass was up, and we'd made
enough makeshift barriers like this,
we could turn the horse out, and buy a cow.

When the time came for proper fencing
you'd saw a log into fencepost lengths
and split them with a maul and wedges.

Not every type of wood was suitable –
put rimu in the ground, for example,
and after five years you could knock it over.

Totara was best, but not a lot grew there;
mostly we had to use hinau: long-lasting,
but fibrous – it wouldn't split cleanly.

You'd knock in wedges, and halfway down the log
meet a cross-fibre snagging it together;
hack through that, more wedges, more knots –

it was half splitting and half chopping.
That was my weekend job year after year,
all the time we were bringing in new land.'

1 ton of no 8 gauge plain wire.
Completed 1 mile = 80 chains of fence.
1 cwt makes 26 chains plain.
1 cwt barbed makes 24 chains.

[Staples, nails and tools not included.]

This Lovely Glen

If, as the story went, it was Eva
who first had the yearning for New Zealand,

perhaps the faintest flicker of a hint
can be extracted from her card to Sam

written 'whilst walking through this lovely Glen,
today thursday is grand, you could [two goes,

neither of them correct, at *'imagine'*]
it was the middle of summer Cyril

send his love and he wonders what you are
doing and who is geting your dinners...'

The Fairy Glen was at Colwyn Bay, her
favourite resort where she, much alone,

while Sam worked night and day, went with their boy
on holiday. He played with other boys

on the shrubby slopes near their boarding house.
She walked and dreamed, dare we guess, of forests –

with gravel paths and a small bridge, perhaps
(or is that me, tidying up her dream

to match the scene on the postcard? If so
I take it back. Let her dream her own dreams.)

But how much, once they were on their mountain,
she walked in the landscape they had purchased

is hard to guess. A saunter now and then
around the farm on a summer evening

at Sam's persuasion would not surprise me,
but that she might have made her way alone

(the children at school, bread baked, hens fed, and
no urgent tasks pressing for the moment)

into the moist huddle of the bush to
peer and listen: that would be something else.

Migrants

There had been precedents: not just Alice,
adventuring across the globe to cure
the 'ailments' her father quailed from naming,

or Eva's cousins in Auckland, or Sam's
'Bro Joe', stumped in Australia: 'The men
will not work and the horses have fell bad'.

Further back there were Sam's Aunt Mary and
her husband, Mormon converts, embarking
under sail on the first part of their trek

to the Salt Lake Valley, or Promised Land.
The first afternoon out from Liverpool,
in a storm, their five-month-old baby died.

The Saints were all prostrate with sea-sickness –
not a woman on board able to stand;
the three Elders had to lay the child out

and stitch her into a sack for the deep,
while Mary writhed in her bunk, clutching her
emptied stomach and full-to-bursting breasts.

Nothing would be worse than this. On they went,
landing in New York, crossing the Great Plains
with Captain Homer Duncan's wagon train –

the wagons being to carry the tents
and baggage, the sick and the very young:
Mary and Thomas and their two boys walked,

their feet festering with poisoned blisters,
a thousand and thirty miles; and what with
diarrhoea and mountain fever and

nervous glances at Indians and wolves,
it was as well they had 'Come, come, ye Saints'
(accompanied on the accordion

around smelly fires of buffalo chips
that the women gathered in their aprons)
to ignite their zeal if it grew tepid.

*

Or, for someone duller, Cousin Joseph,
who waited for the age of the steamship,
zipped across the Atlantic in ten days

to the Pennsylvanian textile trade,
and set Polly, aged 10, and Lizzie, 12,
to earn their livings in a woollen mill.

A Manchester Child

I

Eva's father, Cyril's Grandpa, pierced by
some reminiscent look about the boy,
some aching resemblance, warned them that they

'mustn't try his brain too soon'. What nonsense
to us who know the word 'meningitis'
and that it's an infection, not induced

by arithmetic or learning to read;
who didn't watch that other six-year-old,
Eva's brother, boiling with 'brain fever'

through an endless week of August, and on,
on well into September, to die on
that wilted cliché, Friday the 13th.

II

Too delicate for school, was he? He learned
the strength of the meek: kept them hovering
at the table while he inscribed patterns
into squares of cooling mashed potato.

Sunday school they permitted; it was not
thought to excite the brain too much. At home,
hidden from school inspectors, he picked up
such skills as he could in Grandpa's workshop.

He broke his leg once, playing in the street
with some boys who had a pram-wheeled trolley.
'Tell Daddy he must stick it together
with some jam', wrote Alice from New Zealand.

III

The round-faced, round-eyed lad in a lace-edged
travesty of a sailor collar, with
Norfolk jacket, knickerbockers and clogs,

is seven at last, more than ready to
clop along pavements to Lewis Street School
and begin guzzling up education.

In winter the steel segs on toe and heel
freeze to the snow; he has to pause, and knock
clumps of ice from his soles. Five years later

it is his pony that goes out steel-shod.
No one says this child is too delicate
to ride to school barefoot in rain or sleet.

IV

You couldn't go on being called Cyril,
a name designed only to please parents.
At Te Rauamoa School he got 'Squirrel' –

not that such a mammal existed there
where the chief introduced pests were rabbits,
but the curriculum teemed with fauna

wriggling or scuttling through the imported
literature, snorting in a ballad
or growling in a folk tale. (Euro-what?)

A human compatriot of Kipling
was apparently acceptable too,
even before his accent had flattened.

Baggage

Sealed in their heavy luggage in the hold
they'd brought the encapsulated highlights
of their shed lives: Eva's sewing machine
and her Watteau Doulton dinner service;
Sam's tools, of course; the tea urn his father
had made using his skills as a tinsmith,
learnt in the packing-case trade; some books; the
postcard album bulging with eight or nine
years of miniature correspondence;
and the oval portrait, painted in her
sixties, of Sam's apple-cheeked grandmother
Mary Adcock, née Pell (or perhaps Peel),
in her plaid shawl, who came out of nowhere.

As for the books, they ranged in weight down from
the Bible through Sam's other sacred text,
The Amateur Carpenter and Builder,
to a pocketbook-sized sliver: *Hoyle's Games.*
Packed side by side with Sunday school prizes
(*John Cotton…A New Temperance Tale of
Lancashire Life*) was something different:
*The Awful Disclosures of Maria
Monk* (convent, nuns, dead babies): a dollop
of bigotry for the new country – which
had its own – and an unexpected read
for a bemused future grandchild to pluck
from the glass-fronted bookcase Sam would build.

Celebrations

Mr Adcock has just completed his new house, and a few days ago the settlers tendered him a surprise party.

WAIPA POST, 19 September 1916.

The party was set up by the Dayshes
and included a farewell to their son,
home on final leave, Trooper Hector Daysh:
his health, says the report, 'was drunk with cheers'.

And what was it drunk in? The King Country
was a dry area; any liquor
had to be smuggled in, meekly disguised
as cattle medicine or paint thinner.

Not that a drop of it would have entered
Sam's mouth, Son of Temperance as he was.
He liked a party, though, and best of all
a party at which he could make a speech.

This was in that happy category:
he thanked Mr and Mrs Daysh for their
great kindness to a new arrival from
the Old Country, and gave them a present –

or 'made them a presentation', as the
Waipa Post has it; presentations were
big in the reported social doings
of the settlers at Te Rauamoa.

When Mr Bebbington, the carpenter,
and his wife were off to Te Kuiti,
Sam contributed some witticisms
about the Te Kuitian character,

and another presentation occurred.
The next surprise party we hear about
was for the Dasslers, Oscar and Susan,
at their house. A number of songs were sung;

Mrs Murrell had brought her violin.
Mr Adcock (who else?) paid a tribute
to the host and hostess, and all joined in
singing 'For they are jolly good fellows'.

The School

The school was a wooden box on a hill,
surrounded by weather (the day began
with whose turn it was to check the rain gauge
and read the barometer). It contained
twenty or so children – a family –
and Mr Rudolf Honoré, who would
hand you a slate and teach you your letters,
get you through your Proficiency, or find
Latin inside his head, if by some chance
you had higher aims than agriculture.

Nothing wrong with farming – all his pupils
were from farms – but there was more to be learnt
by those who were keen. *Multum in parvo*:
it was all in that one room, and that one
consciousness, or he'd direct you to it
and make you want to pass it on: outside
the standard lessons, more books to pursue,
more discoveries to seduce you, and
an occasional spring of pure knowledge –
not all science needs laboratories.

Think of seeing his demonstration with
a magnetised needle pushed through a cork
and floating in a basin of water;
or a strip of newspaper: twist it once,
paste the ends together, and cut along
the centre with scissors, and along, and
along, until there's no more 'along': just
one double-length loop; then cut along the
centre of this – and look at what you get!
It makes your brain wriggle inside your skull.

Mr Honoré

Famous in the district for burying
his piano to save it from the flames
when the bush fire of 1908 came
ravening over Te Rauamoa,

(there had been time, clearly, to dig a pit),
he put his dairy farm up for sale and
went off as teacher and (£10 a year
extra) Marine Department signalman

at Marokopa, further down the coast,
a district briefly pullulating with
children after the sawmill opened (though
not a place you hear much about these days),

where he was praised for the 'rapid strides made
especially by the Native children' –
the missionary blood of his Danish
Huguenot grandfather warm in his veins.

In 1913, this time with a wife,
he was back in Te Rauamoa, where
he took over the school from Miss Ashby
and stepped into the role awaiting him.

This too was not without a piano.
After chairing the euchre committee
in support of patriotic wartime
causes (top trophies for the card players:

a handsome palm-stand or a framed picture)
he set about raising funds to buy a
piano for the hall. A nail-driving
contest for ladies was one of his schemes.

This begged-and-nagged-for public piano
was destined, like his own, to be buried,
but permanently and by the long slow
inadvertent smothering of neglect.

District News: Te Rau-a-moa

(Own Correspondent)

A successful school concert was held in the hall last Friday. It was known that for some time past teachers and pupils were actively engaged in preparing for the annual concert, which proved the event of the year. The programme consisted of "A Dolly Show" by seven little girls; the mystic drama "Aladdin and the wonderful lamp", and a musical selection by "ten little nigger boys".

The costumes of the players and the scenery for the four acts of the play were a credit to the senior pupils and the ladies of the district. Master Arthur Ormsby personated the Chinese emperor, and caused much merriment. Miss Gladys Oxenham looked every inch a Princess, quite winning the hearts of the audience, as did also Miss Rene Stewart, the dancing sprite. The difficult role of the wicked magician was cleverly acted by Miss Madge Parkinson.

The leading character and hero of the play was personated by Master Cyril Adcock, whose abilities much impressed the audience. Miss Amy Parkinson, the senior girl of the school, carried out her part as Aladdin's mother with marked confidence and skill, as did also little Dossie Dassler, the maid in waiting to the Princess. Master Bertie Daysh, in a suit of flame, was the second dancing sprite.

The performance was concluded by the ten little nigger boys, whose attire and general appearance amused all and won an encore.

Waipa Post, 29 December 1916

The School Journal

Children of the Empire, you are brothers all;
children of the Empire, answer to the call!
Let your voices mingle, lift your heads and sing:
'God save dear old Britain, and God save Britain's King.'

NZ SCHOOL JOURNAL, Part I, June 1917.

I

There was Empire Day and then Arbor Day,
with a special number of the Journal
for each: you could take it home and file it
in your folder at the end of the year.

'Your teachers will tell you wonderful things
about the British Empire – your Empire,
where children are safe, happy and free.
Some have red skins and live in Canada;

some have black skins and dwell in the land of
the lion and elephant...' No room here
for the 'half-starved savages' wandering
in Australia when the white man came.

However, for something closer to home,
in the section aimed at younger children,
you can read a Maoriland Fairy-tale,
learn a new song to welcome the sunshine,

or find suggestions for a charming pet
in the series on baby animals.
But if you fancy a tuatara
for the back garden you'll need a permit.

II

History, geography and civics
in monthly age-related servings, on
war-time paper, with an occasional
garnish of literature or music –

in between 'Great Rivers of the World'
and the latest strand in 'Britain's Sea Story',
a particularly manly portrait
of Byron, with extracts from 'Childe Harold';

or, for the older age-groups, a report
on the February Revolution
(two months after it occurred), followed by
'The Minstrel Boy' in sol-fa notation.

But when it comes to moulding youthful minds
there's nothing like a polar explorer,
and with the Antarctic so close, guess who
impressed the most readers as top hero?

One, at least, assumed him decades later
to be a universal marker for
moral excellence: 'I'm sure Captain Scott
wouldn't have bullied his little sister.'

Fruit

1916. July 25 Fruit trees – £1.10.0, Paid.

Even in Manchester the first thing you'd plant
in the merest apron of soil was a fruit tree.

So here in the land of milk and honey
it went without saying, didn't it? No.

1,200 feet above sea level
on the chillier side of a mountain

was not ideal; and the soil 'bush-sick' –
deficient in cobalt, as later tests

were to reveal (not wonderful, either,
it also emerged, for dairy cattle).

Grace Dassler, who must nevertheless have
thriven there, spoke aged 102

of empty, bladder-like plums that fell off
before they could ripen. The Dayshes' trees

managed an ill-favoured apple or two,
but for Sam it was dearth. He had to wait

a generation to mellow into
the grandfather I knew when I was five,

a deaf man in his sixties, living near
Drury, to be looked for in a greenhouse

pungent with tomato plants, or peering
through sun-warmed lushness from an orchard ladder,

warning us in a Lancashire accent
not to lick the spray off the nectarines.

34

Mount Pirongia Surveyed

If men in boots had tramped the sacred mountain,
laden with metal implements, compass in hand,
field glasses dangling, puncturing the soil with
the tripod legs of their theodolite stand,
despising the word *tapu* in favour of terms
like 'locked native reserve' and 'second-class land',

deploying their chains to measure slopes of bush
in Anglo-Saxon acres, perches and rods,
reducing ridge and valley to lines on a map,
offering the most perfunctory of nods
to the legal hotch-potch that had been fiddled up
and no respect at all to the ancient gods,

and if then the government had raffled off blocks
and seeded the place with imported farmers, versed
in the wrong kind of animal husbandry,
while spurning the just claimants who were there first,
is it surprising that at least now and then,
here and there, some of it might turn out to be cursed?

The Obvious Solution

A year after the house-warming party
and Sam's off to live in a town again –
or is that a heartless way to put it?

Three words in the diary – 'Came to Dwen' –
commemorate the inadequacy
of the monthly cream cheque to keep them all.

If this is failure, it's temporary
(he hopes), and well-stocked with compensations.
He's packed his kit: razors, razor-strop, comb,

scissors and clippers. He can see himself
reflected in Mr Dwen's tall mirrors
discussing the war as he trims a beard

and clips the back of a customer's neck,
or wielding his less than hilarious
brand of humour while selling tobacco.

He can smell the bay rum he'll spray from his
'ENOTS' plated brass canister. Cyril
has his head screwed on; he'll cope with those cows.

Milk

The thing is to have two milking stools,
one to sit on, the other for your book;

while your hands are busy under a cow,
your eyes and brain can employ themselves elsewhere,

because what is there to think about milk?
The essence of being a mammal, yes,

(these four teats), the image of whiteness –
'He's set her on his milk white steed'.

'Now droops the milkwhite peacock like a ghost'.
'The holly bears a berry as white as the milk' –

(although it's not perfectly white until skimmed);
but day after day, month after month,

ping, ping, ping, swish, ping, swish, ping, swish,
and the foam level crawling up the bucket...

Mum comes out to turn the separator;
I take the can of cream down to the road

for the cream carrier, because the point of it all
is not milk but cream, and not cream, in the end,

but a manufactured product; and in winter
when the cows are dry, all but the house cow,

the dairy company will give us
a 50 lbs box of it for ourselves.

The Bush Fire

There was his wife with her eyebrows burnt off
(they never did grow back again properly)
and his barely teenaged son, running round
with wet sacks to batter the flames out –

just what Sam would himself have advised
if he'd been there, instead of standing
miles and miles away, scissors in hand,
outside the barber's at Te Awamutu,

watching the smoke. (They had no telephone.)
Someone had to go and earn money
when the cream-cheque failed, and someone (young Cyril)
had to mind the farm and milk the cows.

So he missed it, poor Sam, the great bush fire –
the striding flames and the filthy black swirls
that choked you even through a wet handkerchief.
Eva was left with a lasting phobia,

Cyril with an intimate knowledge
of how each type of bush timber burns,
and Sam deprived of a first-hand claim
to a first-class story for his customers.

Beryl

They don't mention her much, but there she was:
running around under Eva's feet;
a smudged face in a family snap,
a bundle of pale skirts on someone's knee –

part of the human baggage they all stowed
as kindly as they could, after Alice
met them from the boat: fair shares;
her whole life accidental.

And growing bigger, taking Cyril's place
in the milking shed after he left home;
complaining of the snow on her feet; standing
in the pool where a cow had piddled to warm them.

Cousins

And then if Beryl why not Hazel? –
who came for some schooling when she was six,

there being no school near Okere Falls.
Cyril took her each day on his pony.

Beryl, too young to have it explained
(even if, in that household,

explanations had been on offer),
thought herself Cyril's sister, not Hazel's –

or Clifford's, who arrived aged six
a year later; Bert from up the road

joined Cyril, each of them ferrying
a small passenger on his saddle.

These were the two handsome children
in careful, slightly too large outfits

(her pleated skirt and sailor collar,
his home-tailored jacket and shorts)

with bare feet on a sunlit verandah.
Beryl is not in the photograph.

What variety of pastoral is this?
A temporary one; as are they all.

Telegraphese

Young woman with TB sails to NZ,
finds work up and down both islands until
near Wanaka she lands up on farm
with no other women; worst happens.

Decent young farmer in neighbourhood
marries her, greatly pregnant. She gives birth
in Dunedin, miles from scowling gaze
of his mother and sisters; brings child home.

Has another, a son, with husband.
Conceives a third. Meanwhile, in Manchester,
her widowed father dies. Husband pays
for her to visit surviving kin.

Staying with brother and sister-in-law
while all make plans to start new life
together in South Island, she hears
Charlie, her husband, has died of typhoid.

Rushes back to claim inheritance,
leaving new baby and toddler behind
with Sam and Eva, and taking only
eldest child: not her husband's. Bad choice.

In-laws refuse to honour Charlie's will.
Alice, whom they see as scarlet woman,
must fend for herself. Finds housekeeping job
with kind widower and his small daughter.

Sam and Eva, en route to Dunedin,
must disembark at Wellington, travel
north to meet them, and reassign children
on rational basis. All their lives change.

The Family Bible

This is the Adcock family Bible:
a wedding present, no doubt, to John and
Amelia in 1870.

The Authorised Version, massively bound
in boards and black leather, with gilt edges,
it runs to over 1200 pages

and weighs between ten and eleven pounds:
as much as a thriving two-month-old child
(not the most tactful of analogies).

Annotations and footnotes occupy
roughly two thirds of the page areas;
maps and engravings bulk the volume out.

Between the Old and New Testaments are
pages for 'Children', 'Marriages' and 'Deaths',
interleaved with crisping tissue paper:

Laura, who died aged one year seven months;
Thomas Henry, who died aged eight months; John
who lived for twenty-one years, but damaged;

then Samuel, to whom the book devolved
as the oldest surviving son, although
not, finally, the only survivor –

Polly, Joseph, George and Alice followed
(as well as another short-lived baby)
before Amelia's death was entered.

Sam is reported to have told his wife
he didn't want children. In this he failed:
Eva's parched womb ignored the edict and,

thirsty for insemination after
seven years of chaste betrothal, conceived
Cyril within their first week of marriage.

His is the only name to represent
his generation on the 'Children' page.
(Nieces fostered and then disowned don't count.)

Bush Fairies

What am I permitted to write about Beryl,
a bright child who wandered into darkness?
Among the squalor in her room when she died
were all the poems she'd written since childhood,

from Bush Fairies, 'weeping for their comrades
slain by an axeman's hand', to her lament
for two infant daughters, a still-born son,
and the young husband she'd nursed for eight years.

If no one quite tells you who you are
how can you decide who you ought to be?
A superfluity of mothers can't prevail
over an Irishman met at a dance.

So: *'Mr and Mrs S. Adcock
announce the engagement of their niece...'*
(previously known, you may recall,
even to herself, as their daughter).

What can you expect if you disgrace yourself
with a consumptive Catholic who drinks?
(Beryl wrote that he took ill from sitting
night after night on his daughter's grave.)

Too much melodrama for Sam and Eva:
need she have lost quite so many babies,
or lain in hospital, coughing and bewailing?
They had seen more than enough TB.

They did their duty: took on the four-year-old
and farmed out the older two; Beryl came home
(streptomycin had been discovered)
and struggled to imitate a mother.

It all dragged on as you might expect:
some lodger, not always the same one,
drinking beer with her in the front room
and listening to the racing commentary;

the sensible daughter coping with the chores
until her turn for a rapid wedding.
And then...but all right: it's not my business.
Let me apologise if I've already

bumbled clumsily into the peace
of the living. And might it not have been
more tactful to give Beryl a new name? –
Assuming, that's to say, that I haven't.

Settlers' Museum

The early settlers' museum echoes
to voices chiming 'We had one of those!'
So did we, folks: we all had one of those –
washboard, washing dolly, Reckitt's bluebag,
scrubbing brush, sandstone, bar of Sunlight soap –
or our mother did, or our grandmother.
Surely you've got a wash-house out the back
with a copper in it, and a mangle?
Oh, just the copper; you sold the mangle
on Trade-Me or, more likely, wish you had.

The kitchen from a hundred years ago
combines the boringly familiar –
fireguard, hearth brush, poker, shovel, tongs –
with the no longer seen: a butter churn,
that pair of flatirons (one to heat up
on the range while the other's being used),
the black kettle – and is that a trivet?
A side of bacon hanging from a beam;
Willow pattern china brought from England,
and tea-towels made out of flour bags.

In the display the aproned figure posed
amid the props ('Farmhouse Interior')
is visible only in half profile,
busy at the table about some task –
kneading bread, perhaps. It's not possible
to view her from another angle, or
tiptoe around behind the barrier
to ask her name and peer into her face.
The teapot's just like ours. The milk jug has
a bead-fringed net cover (my aunts used those).

Evenings with Mother

As there was only one lamp
they had to spend the winter evenings
at the table, close enough to share
its kerosene-perfumed radiance –

his mother sewing, and he
reading aloud to her the books
he borrowed from Mr Honoré
or the Daysh boys on the next farm:

Buffalo Bill, school yarns from
England (*Talbot something of the Shell*),
and, featuring his own personal
hero, *Deerfoot in the Mountains*.

(Deerfoot rode Whirlwind bareback
without a bridle. His own pony,
Molly, would go anywhere like this,
but Kate, the harness mare, threw him off.)

Their six-volume Walter Scott
absorbed them both for weeks and could then
be swapped with the Dassler family
for Dickens or (why not?) Billy Bunter.

But his mother's attention
may have wandered when his own was gripped,
in a stack of old *Boy's Own Papers*,
by details of wireless telegraphy.

The Buggy

(Cyril speaks)

Mum wasn't much of a one for horses.
If she needed to go out anywhere
she had to be taken in the buggy.

Sometimes I drove her, when Dad was away;
otherwise he did, but he wasn't keen:
it had four high wheels, awkward to manage

(we used it for transporting loads); and Kate,
our heavier mare, built like a draught horse,
was such a timid, skittish animal,

a bag of nerves. Well, one day Mum had gone
to Otorohanga with the Dayshes,
and I was to follow in the buggy.

I got Kate harnessed and between the shafts,
the fidgety creature, and all went well
until she saw something she didn't like –

possibly something imaginary.
She reared up, tipped me out into the mud,
jack-knifed the wheels, and trotted off at a

great pace back towards home. There was never
any traffic on that road, thank goodness,
but about a mile and a half downhill

a man working on the verge spotted her,
buggy in tow, and managed to hold her
until I caught up and took her in charge.

We made it in the end – no harm done – but
if Mum had been with me, I dread to think...
although at least it would have given her

something to write about in letters home
to friends in Manchester (where there were trams);
if she'd been more of a one for writing.

Eight Things Eva Will Never Do Again

Work in that dressmaking factory,
waiting for Sam to marry her. (He had
duties, and a curious conscience.)

Walk out with him along Peel Green Road
to the Ship Canal bridge, on a May evening
with the hawthorn in flower – if he could snatch time
from his two jobs – or after church, perhaps.
(Seven years of that, walking out together.)

Go home and make clothes for her sisters.
(Someone had to, and you wouldn't catch
Mary lifting a hand around the house.)

Help her mother with whatever (ditto).

Stand in the New Independent Chapel
(a concession by Sam, who is C of E),
sheathed in white, with a pearl choker,
and balancing on her head a cushion
of ostrich feathers, to murmur her vows.

Go to Blackpool. (Everyone loves Blackpool.)
'Dear Sam, Sorry you was dispointed...
Tell Marion to bring a shall for her head
as we are expecting high tide on Sunday
and give her mine to bring. You will find it
in the bottom draw in the parlor...'

See Marion, or others of her younger
siblings (names available on request).

Have a baby. (Well, she has Cyril.)

Eva Remembers Her Two Brothers Called James

When she thinks (if she does) of the first James
it is of a six-year-old who died
when she was fourteen, of meningitis.

His spirit, like a trespassing sprite,
flew into his parents' marriage bed
and lurked there as they comforted each other.

A month later, conspiring with the genie
of ovulation and the hormone fairies,
it implanted itself in a fertilised egg,

to be born in July 1890
and loaded with the same eight syllables:
James Arthur Dickson Eggington.

He didn't resemble his first avatar
or any of his incarnate siblings
at Eva's wedding, this gladsome imp

with his long chin. When TB clutched him
'I am still improving', he wrote
from his sanatorium in Devon

on a photograph of six young men
reclining on the grass around a nurse
like petals flopped from a magnolia.

James is the one with the longest legs,
the centre parting, the fetching moustache,
and no intention of dying celibate.

He willed some health back into his lungs,
found work, tacked five years on to his age,
and married an older woman while he could.

How's that for *carpe diem*? Ten months
to bask in matrimony, wisely or not,
before death stalked him to Babbacombe.

Eva Remembers Her Little Sisters

'Alice Maud Mary, Marion Maud Mary,
Ellen Gertrude (the first), Ellen Gertrude Mary –

all us girls got Mary, after our mother,
starting with Mary Ann Elizabeth, then me –

all but one, that is, the first Ellen Gertrude,
and perhaps it was bad luck to have left it off;

she had the shortest life: only nine months old
when she took fits and died (it was pneumonia).

But the first we lost was my playmate Alice:
eight when I was ten. *Tabes mesenterica* –

something internal; a horrible complaint.
It wasn't the way they tell you at Sunday school.

She died ten days after Marion was born.
It was all like that: steps and stairs and overlaps,

birthdays and deathdays and the names given again,
almost as if there was something to cover up.

When Marion took bad our brother Thomas
carried her around the house in his arms...

Them pictures they made us pose for, in our mourning,
Nellie and me, before it was too late –

time enough left for me, but not for Nellie,
poor lass, with her shy smile, a bit bucktoothed,

her hair tied back with a black satin bow
in front of the photographer's painted scenery...

God forgive me, I'd rather have kept Nellie
than Mary with her snooty ways, or Thomas,

if there was only room left on this earth
for four of us out of the eleven.'

51

The Germans

I

From our front window we could peer down
at Kawhia Harbour, a quiet place,
ideal for the Germans to land. I indulged
in fantasies, but with an undercurrent.

An unknown farmer moved in next door:
a spy, obviously. The boundary between
us and the spy needed quite a length of fencing.
I don't know when I've worked so hard on a fence.

II

My Uncle Harry, Mum's youngest brother,
was invalided home from the Somme
with something...rheumatic fever, they thought –
his heart was enlarged. Or perhaps he had

shellshock. His mother dared not nurse him:
the responsibility unnerved her.
Instead his sister-in-law volunteered,
Thomas's wife. She said he had fits.

Brown Sugar

(Cyril speaks)

The teacher's brother, Charlie Honoré,
had a farm close to the school, and also
fingers in other pies from time to time.
He managed the boarding house for a bit,
and even talked of opening a store.

He wouldn't miss an opportunity –
like the day when he distinguished himself
by running three-quarters of a mile to
grab the mail coach, when the horses bolted.
He got himself in the paper for that.

When he hired me to help with his milking
I'd get up in the dark, milk my own cows,
ride two miles to Charlie's place and milk his,
then go to school. But he gave me breakfast,
and boy, was I ready for that porridge!

At Charlie's house it came with brown sugar –
he said raw sugar was better for you.
Everyone had porridge for breakfast,
but I'd never had brown sugar before;
so I persuaded Mum to get some in.

Later, of course, I learned it was better
to have no sugar at all; later still
I gave up cooking the oats, and simply
soaked them overnight in a mug of milk –
a sort of predecessor to muesli.

Supporting Our Boys

I

Syd Ormsby put his stock up for auction,
announcing his departure for the front,
but didn't even get as far as camp
before the armistice overtook him –

bad luck or procrastination? Others
enlisted straight away: 'Anzac hero'
John Linwood did his bit and died at (where
else?) Gallipoli in 1915.

Charlie Honoré, at the farewell for
Trooper Dassler of the Mounted Rifles,
urged all the single men to volunteer
before the arrival of compulsion.

Whatever the impetus, off they marched –
names from the school roll: Smith, Clark, Dearlove, Daysh;
three from the Harris family (only
one survived); two Parkinsons; two Franklins.

In 1917 the *Waipa Post*
bemoaned the shortage of dairy farmers,
noting that fern and other second growths
were creeping into neglected pastures,

and tried to imagine the effects when
the second reserve came to be called up,
since already most of the remaining
settlers were married men with families.

Following his own call to arms, Charlie
Honoré detached himself from his wife,
his businesses, his farm, his committees,
and sailed off with the next reinforcements.

In time it would have gobbled them all up.
It even came snapping at Sam's heels, in
August 1918, with the 16th
ballot, but was just too slow to snatch him.

II

Thirty or thereabouts went; all but five
came back, some in better shape than others –
young Ned Honoré spent two years dying
in Trentham military hospital.

Max Dassler was invalided home from
Egypt after serving scarcely a year,
and settled with other returned soldiers
on the Tapuohonuku block; there,

having something to prove, he was shortly
'bringing his place under in record time'.
His brother Oscar, with no such resource,
turned to the law when accused of stealing

a bag of potatoes; the magistrate,
awarding £10 damages, took note
of the ill feeling caused since war broke out
by his being 'of foreign extraction'.

Meanwhile returned Gunner Stewart, with his
war record and impeccable surname,
continued to act as cheerleader and
auctioneer at the fundraising socials.

Armistice Day

He was fourteen when it ended.
His father gave him a day off
to ride into town for the celebrations.

Ambling along on Molly's back
to Te Awamutu, he whiled away
the miles absorbed in his new treasure:

a textbook on organic chemistry,
saved up for out of his earnings
from doing Charlie Honoré's milking.

After the fireworks, his retina stencilled
with their acidic blaze, he wondered
how easy it would be to make some.

He might have a go, with Bert Daysh,
assuming they could get the ingredients
(or get away with trying to get them;

he could hardly add them to his parents'
next routine order from Laidlaw Leeds
for oatmeal, sugar and fencing wire).

They could celebrate the New Year, perhaps,
or the King's birthday – he'd think of something –
now that there would be no more wars.

The Way Forward

I

Mr Honoré came and spoke to Dad;
I'm not sure how the conversation went,

but the gist of it was that I shouldn't
waste my life being a dairy farmer.

There was no chance of going to high school –
I'd have had to give up work on the farm,

which at that stage could barely totter on.
As for university, forget it.

The path to higher education lay
through training as a teacher, like himself.

First the civil service entrance exam,
then probationer (or pupil teacher,

as they once called it); then training college.
And I'd be paid; I'd be self-supporting.

II

I stayed on at school to Standard 7
and Mr Honoré gave me coaching

in Latin and some other new subjects
for the entrance exam. Not the maths, though –

by then I think I knew about as much
maths as he did; once when he was teaching

contracted multiplication and got
a bit stuck, I helped him from the textbook.

After a few months I left; from then on
packets of correspondence course lessons

would arrive from T.U. Wells in Auckland
for me to complete and post back to him.

I drew up a timetable for myself;
I was a sort of self-governing school.

The Hopeful Author

The professor in 'A Scientific
Capture', with the detective by his side,
effects an entry into the spy's house
by lassooing a chimney, shinning up
the rope and removing a window pane.

He installs his first 'little contrivance'
(a glass-lidded box) behind a mirror,
and another under the wallpaper,
each connected to the telephone wire
and then in turn to a large battery

outside the house. Then (are you still with me?)
back in the professor's lab they can watch
the villain's dastardly doings on a
'cinnamatagraph', but one which can play,
unlike commercial models, a soundtrack.

All very advanced, like the 'flying tank'
of which the prototype has been stolen
by the spy. To ratchet up the tension,
when they are on their way to arrest him
the detective's car runs out of benzine.

It all works out as it should in the end:
more wires, another battery, the spy
electrocuted at his own front door.
On the back of the much-creased final page:
C. Adcock. Remit U.S. Bills & stamps.

A Friend of the New

(Cyril speaks)

'One disadvantage of the coherer
is its erratic nature; it's not
a reliable signalling device.'

In Auckland, I had a crystal set,
and made a valve receiver.
But I'm talking about the early days:

to begin with I experimented
with iron filings and nitric acid –
I'd read it all up. Meanwhile Bill Daysh,

Bert's brother, took some wire out of an old
telephone, I bought a little buzzer,
and we made Morse keys, and sent signals

from his house to ours. They were hard to pick up.
We stretched our ears to distinguish them;
there was some imagination involved.

But we got a tremendous kick out of
picking up signals from Awanui –
ZLA Awanui, in Northland;

hadn't a notion of what they were saying.
Of course there was no speech in those days,
only Morse; nothing but Morse in the air.

Shorthand

Might you not have found him a little
exhausting, though? If, for example,
you were his mother, not given

to innovative thinking yourself,
and had this youth (in 1920
the word teenager was not current),

forever coming up with a new
interpretation of *Genesis*
or sketching plans for a contraption

that must be at least electrical,
if not dangerous. And now this:
a small ad in the *Auckland Star* –

SHORTHAND in three hours. New system,
easily learned. Send 5/- for
course. C. Adcock, Te Rau-a-moa.

That was in June; but on reflection
three hours may have struck him as less than
five shillings' worth. So in December:

SHORTHAND in three days. Write C. Adcock
regarding the Veasy system...
Oh, yes, ha ha – Veasy: v. easy.

Did you make any money, Cyril?

The Bible Student

Dad was very thick with the Anglicans
in Te Awamutu. We had no church
at Te Rauamoa, but once or twice a year
a man came to take a church service.
There was one time when he couldn't make it
and I volunteered. (Don't look so surprised!)
Dad found someone else for the routine parts
of the service, but I preached the sermon:
my first experience of public speaking.
I was about fifteen, I suppose.

I can't remember what the text was.
I'd been reading a chapter of the Bible
every night, starting with Genesis.
We all had Bibles; Dad's was annotated –
I studied it for the notes – but mine
was the Revised Version; I was adamant
about sticking to the Revised Version.
Then I got the 'Emphatic Diaglott' –
the New Testament in the original Greek
with an interlined English translation.

Also I somehow managed to get hold of
Pastor Russell's six-volume study.
This appealed to my rebellious mind
(I was never happy to take on trust
what I'd been told). He wrote, for example,
that hell was not a place of torment at all:
the Old Testament word meant simply
a place of oblivion, and Gehenna,
the New Testament word, was a place
of disposal: a rubbish tip, you could say.

I was quite voluble on scriptural matters! –
I always enjoyed a good argument.
When they set up a Sunday school,
with me and an older girl as teachers,
the children must have heard some new viewpoints;
I don't imagine it did much damage
to their immortal souls. Later on,
in Auckand, I taught at the Ridgeways' church.
Which denomination? I forget; by then
I'd no time for such petty distinctions.

A Profile

Was he a rather solemn young person?
– There is nothing to contradict that view.
Was he, on the other hand, often filled
with glee at his own schemes and inventions?
– To say that would be equally valid.
Was anything in the nature of fun
mentioned? – He went out shooting now and then:
rabbits, mostly. Once, with Bert and Bill Daysh,
he hunted some feral cats that had been
skulking and marauding around their farm,
raiding the poultry yard. Never got one.
Did the subject of sex ever arise?
– Come on, this was my father talking to
his daughter and grandson. What do you think?

DISTRICT NEWS: TE RAU-A-MOA

(Own Correspondent)

Master Cyril Adcock, son of Mr S. Adcock of Te Awamutu, is to be congratulated on having passed the civil service entrance examination.

His success is especially pleasing seeing that the youth has been constantly employed on his father's dairy farm here at Te Rauamoa. It shows what can be done by application. The boy intends to enter one of the learned professions.

Of the two candidates presented for junior national scholarships, Dorothea Dassler, eldest daughter of Mr O.P. Dassler, obtained a free place. She has been a constant pupil at the school here, having been trained throughout by the same teacher.

Some fine crops of Swedes are to be seen on the farms round about, the most promising being those grown on virgin land. Conditions are very favourable
for growth, a week's hot weather being invariably followed by copious rains.

Waipa Post, 8 February 1921

Mr S. Adcock

'Mr Adcock of Te Awamutu'
will have to cease being a hairdresser
of that town, toil back up the hill on his
bicycle, live with his wife and resume

the identity of Mr Adcock,
dairy farmer of Te Rauamoa,
so that his son can freewheel down in the
other direction to be a teacher.

If he could somehow stockpile the milking
by having it done ten times in a row
and then not at all for three or four days...
but the cows won't yield until they're ready.

It's time to train Beryl – she's nearly eight,
old enough to start getting her hand in.
He'll have other tasks enough, goodness knows;
it's all coming back to him. So be it,

but he draws the line at cutting firewood.
Cyril will have to cycle home at the
weekends – have a good meal, see his mother.
That's the answer. That's all there is to it.

The Probationer

(Cyril speaks)

I

Quite a shock, the switch to a small township
with streets and shops and traffic and strangers.

I was sixteen, and one of three trainees
appointed to Te Awamutu school.

The District High School was in a newly
opened building, with the primary school;

it specialised in agriculture and,
for girls, home economics (yes, I know).

My own studies enlarged my horizons –
the topics deemed to be necessary

for a teacher ranged from the close parsing
of a sentence to physiology,

hygiene and diet, the sugar question...
It was all very educational.

II

Chemistry was not on my syllabus
but the school science inspector agreed

to let me study it at the high school
one evening a week, designing my own

course of experiments; my friend Bert Fleay
from Te Rahu, a year younger than me

(he was a pupil, I was a teacher)
joined me. Once, for example, we measured

the carbon dioxide in the classroom
after the students had left. I tended

to favour exciting experiments –
lots of burning and electricity,

running fearful wires off the light sockets –
not the routine stuff Bert had done in class.

Te Awamutu Road Rant

You'd see it in your dreams half the night long
afterwards, the road reeling and rolling
in front of you, surging and zigzagging,
hairpin-bending here and there, but slowly –

how could it be fast on a bicycle
except downhill a bit, on the way back,
at Windy Point, for example, where you
might go over if you didn't watch out?

It was twenty-seven miles, which would take
five hours (unless you made the mistake
of going by the back road – that took nine;
once was enough for that experiment).

The first eight miles, from Te Awamutu
to Pirongia, were tolerable;
then came five miles of rough metal – great lumps
this size; you could only ride at the edge.

From there on the rest of it was rough clay,
often waterlogged in the wet season,
which was much of the time: your wheels could glug
through gluey mud as deep as six inches.

It would be raining, as likely as not –
you'd want your oilskin cape, and your leggings
(two and threepence a pair in Laidlaw Leeds'
catalogue, leather or waterproof cloth),

and if you set out late on a Friday
there was also the problem of a light:
a carbide lamp was best, but it wouldn't
last; you'd need an oil lamp as a backup.

(The alternative was to leave early,
on Saturday morning, although it might
be just as dark at 4 or 5 a.m.)
Then all weekend the firewood marathon:

hunting down suitable logs, harnessing
Kate to drag them home; then sawing, chopping,
sawing again, splitting, cutting, stacking –
different types of wood for different

cooking, fast or slow: bread in the oven,
stew on the hob, water in the boiler –
and the range to be kept alight all day
for warmth ten months of the year, gobbling trees.

Monotonous, yes, but not hypnotic.
It was the cycling that would haunt your sleep:
all that swinging around sea-sick curves and
corners, the pedals churning round and round,

the head-down grind; the circularity.
But even if your eyes went round in your
head you'd have to concentrate in case of
tree-roots, loose rocks, deceptively deep ruts.

And back at Te Awamutu you'd still
have three more miles to go to Te Rahu
and your bed in old Hughie Thompson's house;
before the following weekend came round.

The Sensational

I rather suspect there is not enough sex,
murder and cannibalism in these
pages to please such themes' devotees:

no pornographic, priapic or Sapphic
doings on record, no lopping of limbs,
no butchered-out hearts, no roasting of parts,

nothing rococo in the Okoko
Valley, to speak of, as far as I know,
nor within cooee of Ngutunui.

The second and third may well have occurred
a century or two back, in that vast
repository of horrors, the past –

think, after all, of Te Rauparaha
whose first rampages were not very far
down the old coach road, at Kawhia;

and during some war a long time before,
in the days of the moa-hunters, it's said
that after one battle so many dead

were strewn on the ground that they brought to mind
the tumbled mounds of long-legged birds
felled in a moa-hunt; since when the words

'Te Rau-a-Moa' – 'the hundreds like moa' –
have stuck to that place.
                                   As for sex, though,
how would we know? It was all so long ago.

The Kea Gun

I

The rifle known to them as the Kea gun
was so named by Cyril's uncle Charlie,
who used to keep it by him to shoot Kea
when those demonic parrots attacked his sheep.

His widow Alice must have snatched it up
with such goods as she could salvage when
'them wretches at Makarora' (Sam's words)
ignored his Will and threw her off the farm.

(Quite soon whatever need she might have felt
for a gun evaporated; Mr Weir –
he was always Mr Weir – protected her
for the rest of their long lives together.)

The rifle featured in an earlier drama
not known to any of them, and to us
only through smart-arse online indexes:
Charlie, in his teens, had embraced

the age-old solace of lonely shepherds,
and was brought before the Chief Justice
convicted of an unnatural offence.
His Honour, in passing sentence, said:

'...on the other hand, you are only a lad...
strongly recommended to mercy...
brought up away from many comforts...
depraved moral sense...better life in future...'

Six months, with hard labour; and the same,
to be served concurrently, on the charge
of mischievously killing a sheep,
to which he pleaded guilty in the lower court.

Local opinion at Lake Wanaka
was that the charge should never have been brought –
the felony, that is; it was admitted
'that a prosecution in the case

of shooting the ewe with the pea rifle
was unavoidable.' [Semantic interlude:
a pea rifle is a small bore rifle –
a .22. *Pea* rhymes with *key*

but not with *kea*, which has two syllables.
I shan't pronounce on what it might rhyme with.]
The *Otago Witness* was pained to report
that many small children knew all the details

which is more than we do. Why did Charlie
have to shoot the ewe? *Crime passionel?*
Silencing a witness? – Come on now,
pull yourselves together: we're all grown-ups.

II

'Indelicate' and 'speculate' don't rhyme,
any more than Makarora does
with Te Rauamoa. Often a rifle
is used only for keeping down rabbits.

This was not traditional sheep country.
No kea to shoot, and on this farm no sheep.
A herd of dairy cattle can't compete
with a flock of woolly temptresses.

Glamorous though the front end of a heifer
may be (those eyelashes, those melting eyes)
the bovine frame lacks cuddliness, compared
with the compact snugness of a ewe.

When it comes to interspecies relations
(hardly a matter I'm equipped to judge)
a cow seems not only less alluring
but less well adapted to the purpose.

Fortunately for the young man on this farm
(Charlie's nephew by marriage, let's call him)
by the time he reached 17 (the age
at which Charlie made his appearance in court)

he was working at Te Awamutu
District High School, where there were girls.
He went to at least one jazz concert.
There may even have been jazz with girls.

Sole Charge

If people had said 'Wow' in those days
he might have said it, during a visit
to his aunt Alice, when Mr Weir
left him to run the hydroelectric
power station at Okere Falls
for an afternoon: Rotorua
dependent on a boy for its power!

The needle of his ambition swung
from research chemist to electrical
engineer. But his direction
had been set for him already: he was
going to be a teacher; and not
of physics or chemistry; he was going
to teach primary school children.

At Te Uku, his first posting,
he would live in a tent in the school grounds
on rolled oats, peanuts and raw carrots,
and sleep on a palliasse of hay
with another over him for the cold.
He would teach them everything he knew.
They would think him a freak, of course,

but take to him. His evening lectures
would tickle the parents: music (using
his 'non-tin whistle' and the Walford Davies
gramophone records); poetry; art –
always aglow with the latest. He would stick
in their memories. Decimal currency
(you wait – it will come); steam cars; Esperanto.

The Plain and Fancy Dress Ball

The evening of Friday last saw the high-water mark of social
entertainment in Te Rau-a-moa raised to a still higher level...

WAIPA POST, 25 October 1924

I

The 1920s were in full swing.
Eva and Sam went with the Dayshes,

Mrs Daysh in black silk, 'Mrs S.
Adcock' in a silk net over-dress.

Of the thirty-five ladies listed,
(not counting unnamed 'others'), ten wore

fancy dress, and the rest evening dress.
Mrs Le Prou came as a 'Cheer Germ',

Charlie Honoré's wife as a nurse.
(The gentlemen's clothing was not thought

worthy of journalistic comment.)
Mrs Chase, dressed as 'Evening', received

a presentation. People came from
as far away as Pirongia.

II

Meanwhile Cyril, at Training College
in Auckland, cycled every day from

Point Chevalier, where he was boarding
with his mother's cousins the Ridgeways,

in riding-breeches, leggings and boots
with an oilskin cape in wet weather –

a costume similarly favoured
by the previous year's eccentric,

76

his fellow-Esperantist, Watson
(a soul-mate, had they coincided),

and religiously sent home money,
out of which Eva may have bought the

fabric for her outfit at the ball –
or her update to an older frock.

The Swimmer

(Cyril speaks)

Another thing at Teachers' College:
three of us always got in early
to go the length of the swimming bath,
winter or summer, before classes.

On one occasion we got roped in
to a life-saving exhibition.
Yes, I was the victim; I had to
thrash about and pretend to struggle.

I was a fairly small chap, easy
to handle. At that point I hadn't
learnt life-saving – I didn't even
learn to swim till Te Awamutu.

There was a lake at the Thompsons' farm:
they had a bit of bush and a lake
surrounded by raupo: a deep lake –
we never found the bottom of it.

(At Te Rauamoa the only
water was what fell out of the sky,
or the odd stream – nothing to swim in;
the water we used was from our tank.)

Later, of course, I learned life-saving;
I used to teach it to the children
at Rangiwahia – there was a
river nearby – do you remember?

Visiting the Ridgeways

But if they're all in Auckland
standing together in the Ridgeways' garden –
Sam, Eva, Beryl (about ten or eleven)
and grown-up Cyril – then who's milking the cows?

Is the farm over? No, not for a while.
It's Cyril who will unclog them from it,
putting his motorbike down as a deposit
on eight acres in Drury for their rescue.

Meanwhile here they are on a visit:
Eva enduring the camera, Sam tired,
Cyril with his muscular arms folded,
Beryl in a white dress Eva has sewn

as she used to sew for her sisters
in fashions to suit them, during their brief prime.
Likewise this low-belted shift is of its time –
the 1920s – to please Beryl. It's as if

Sam's niece, this unofficial daughter,
were a present for Eva, that might make up
for Nellie and Marion. Oh, too much to hope –
that Eva should enjoy consolation.

Reconstituting Eva

No; I can't get it to knit. Scrunch!
Somewhere on the time-line between
the historical Eva whose
disappointments and retreating
daydreams I so tenderly probe
and our childhood's 'Grandma Adcock'
comes a fracture: Sam's young lady,
eager emigrant, pioneer,
snaps into the dumpy figure
telling me off, when I was three,
for proving, at the tea-table,
I could put my toes in my mouth.

The two images crepitate
against each other, and won't graft.
She showed no signs of liking us,
my sister and me, her only
grandchildren, that we can think of.
No reason why she should, except
that it seems to be usual;
but we visited, ate her stew
and washed the dishes afterwards.
Grandpa was jolly enough, and
we had another grandmother
for normal human purposes.

Eva left us out of her will
because of our shocking morals:
no thoughtful little legacies
'to my beloved granddaughter'.
Disapprobation was her norm
and 'aggrieved' her default status.
How baffled she might look to hear
I've kept her prayer book (the one
she used at Drury, parading
as an Anglican to please Sam).
What's more – no thanks to her – I was
given, years ago, her gold brooch.

Ragwort

Senecio jacobaea: bad news,
this pretty weed, this constellation
of tiny suns, this doomful harbinger.

Farmers have walked off their land for less.
Cattle deficient in minerals
develop 'a depraved appetite' for it.

It springs beaming out of the soil
to seduce yet another silly beast
with its fairy gold. Whoa! Keep off!

But no: there they go, pathetic addicts,
mouthing and sucking at its alkaloids
like Laura at fruit in the goblin market

until they stagger with cirrhosis
while the plants, like all drug pushers,
multiply as fast as you cut them down.

Te Rauamoa got it early:
a present from the Seddon government
for the new settlers, smuggled in

with the grass seed. 'The Golden City',
people sneered in 1905
at the ragwort capital of the North Island,

that straggle of bush clearings, jaundicing
the landscape with their urinous tinge.
The authorities marched in a posse of sheep

to munch the invaders to the ground –
for the moment, that is.
                          My own ragwort moment –
my burning bush – on a childhood holiday

in Kent was a clump of dazzle
braided with matching caterpillars
in yellow and black stripes: the Cinnabar moth,

the designated predator. Next morning,
peering from our tent, I saw them felled.
'Poor little things', I wrote in my nature notebook.

Walking Off

Take the Dasslers, for example: even with
a buggy and two horses they were walking –
leaving it all, turning their backs, quitting

for somewhere closer to sea-level
where they needn't top-dress the soil with cobalt
and their young stock didn't wither away.

But the farm just had to sit there, languishing
for anyone who might wander by and want it,
while ragwort sniggered in the long grass;

and the hall couldn't up and walk off: it lay
under its drooping macrocarpas and wilted,
letting the blackberries crawl over its roof –

the piano is still under the wreckage.
No one revived the Post Office
that Susan Dassler had run in her front room;

the butcher's shop in a hut by the roadside
where you helped yourself and recorded your purchase
in a notebook somehow faded away;

a bus took the children to Ngutunui.
And after all, what else had there been but the hall,
the butcher's shop, the post office and the school? –

wrote Susan Dassler with her 'Pioneer's Pen'.

The Roads Again

The *Waipa Post* correspondent frothing,
nonsensical with rage: 'Our settlement...
the first to be formed in the King Country...
twenty-three years of broken promises –
yet it is without a road'. What he means
is a road better than a muddy track
through the bush; one fit for motor traffic.

The 1890s: ten unemployed men,
one remembered as Old Daddy Hoffman,
another as someone's uncle Dan Coe,
trundled their goods uphill on packhorses
to start clearing two hundred acres each
(donated by Dick Seddon's government)
and build slab huts with doors made of sacking.

Twenty years later it's pit-sawn timber
and windows with proper glass in the frames,
but still no end to the resolutions,
the petitions to the authorities
(in duplicate, the settlement having
the misfortune to straddle two counties),
the jokes about profits for coach-menders;

Mary Scott shuddering her way down the
Pekanui with a two-horse buggy
until her husband has to snatch the reins
to save them both from a gully (she'll learn);
while on the coach road a score of settlers
have made up a party to spread gravel
on the most hazardously washed-out bends.

When the through road no longer grates your bones
or makes your back-seat passengers carsick,
when its crimps and squiggles have been combed out,
angles trimmed off, surface tar-sealed, so that
your car glides like butter on a warm knife,
it will have become just that: a through road
with nothing to stop off for on the way.

The Hall: a Requiem

Bill Daysh and the vicar from Kawhia
on cornet, Mrs Chase on piano,
Stan Gilmour making his violin sing,
someone on drums – the joint must have been jumping.
But that was after the tennis club opened
in the 1930s (and before it closed).

The hall began when one of the settlers
gazed at the dairy factory – defunct
now that they all had separators at home –
and was inspired. They laid a wooden floor
over the concrete, turned the engine room
into a stage and transformed the cool-room.

It served for everything: school concerts,
church services, a wedding now and then...
Cyril taught Sunday school there, but the only
dances he mentions were at Te Uku,
in his twenties. They went on all night
until it was time for the morning milking –

which, as a teacher, he didn't have to do.
He might have married a farmer's daughter
instead of a music teacher from Drury
where she and her friends in the girls' club
made butterfly cakes and Melting Moments
for the suppers at dances in the Drury Hall,

although even then and certainly later
in Sidcup, when they could snatch time out
from their separate shifts during the Blitz
for the First Aid Post New Year's Eve party,
he was always keener on dancing
than the music teacher turned out to be.

Barton Cottage, 1928

I

There was no mistaking it: this
   white stucco-covered box
two stories high, planted firmly
   where you'd expect to see
a weatherboard bungalow or
   traditional villa,
on the corner of eight acres
   of manageable land,
and labelled, when Sam had finished,
   with a name imported,
like the building method, from Home.

The date above the porch
was also on the licences
   for their shotguns – 'Farmer,
Drury', they said firmly (the years
   in Te Rauamoa
barely hinted at on the back) –
   never mind that Cyril
was a teacher at Te Uku;
   this would be Sam, signing
both of them up to the landscape
   his son had found for him.

Having personalised the house
   he began scent-marking
the village (all right, 'the township'):
   opened a hairdressing
kiosk, became a church warden
   at Old St John's, and built
with his own tools and kauri planks
   from the Selwyn cottage
a Sunday school (it stood until
   the road widening); he
was thanked with a barometer.

II

The gloss on this green-streaked apple
    suggests that of a glass
marble, or a healthy eyeball;
    glint is another word,
or gleam, for its wet-look surface.
    It was handed to me
by the present young tenant of
    Barton Cottage, who had
'always wondered about this house'.
    'My grandfather built it',
I said, 'and planted an orchard...'

    Ah, still there. He's walked me
through damp grass to the gnarled trunks, the
    boughs crusty with lichen
but, for the most part, still bearing.
    And the plum trees, he says,
'flood the ground with fruit' in season.
    This waxen globe must be
a Cox's orange pippin, not
    ripe yet; perfect but for
one minute puncture mark that won't
    show in a photograph.

Cyril's Bride

When Cyril brought his bride to live, perforce,
huggermugger with him and his parents,
Eva allowed her new daughter-in-law,
who daily proffered help with the cooking,
daily to make the salad; there was no
other role for her at Barton Cottage –

except, of course, to cosset Cyril from
escaping to an independent life.
(He was not long back from something like that,
camping in the school grounds at Te Uku
with his motorbike and his swotty books –
although guess who got half his salary?)

Aeneas was relieved of Anchises
when Sam and Eva made the big trip Home.
Luck struck: the nearly-local school was closed
and Cyril posted to safely far-flung
Graham's Beach on the Manukau Harbour,
scarcely accessible except by launch.

Freedom set in: baching and making shift,
sleeping out of doors on the verandah
(the uses that man had for a tent-fly!)
rather than smothering in the bedroom
of their rented cottage; reading the minds
of hens that nested half-wild in the bush.

They sold their Austin Seven and bought an
old clinker-built lifeboat, once a whaler's,
which (nobody's fault) stranded them on a
sand bank when they chugged across the harbour
towards Auckland, planning to welcome with
a *fait accompli* their former jailers.

Nostalgia Trip, 1976

He still shared the culture of No 8 fencing wire
in which, for example, Charlie at Makarora
had cut two lengths from that universal resource
to make a pair of knitting needles for Alice.

So Cyril, or John, as his second wife now called him,
finding himself and her and his daughter (the one from
England) and a teenage grandson locked out of the car,
conjured an entry by means of a noose of fuse wire

attached, with the boy's help, to a rod of No 8;
and whether he travelled with wire clippers in the boot
is lost. He had parked near the school at Te Rauamoa,
drawn by a mycelium thread of nostalgia

to that fostering parent, a one-roomed box of tricks
once thrumming with rote-learnt grammar and arithmetic,
with singing lessons, geography and Empire Day,
but now muffled, stuffed up to its rafters with hay.

The Education Board carpenter skimped on the timber
in 1897 – kauri would have cost more
than mountain rimu, which nevertheless outlived
the building's function and stood firm until we arrived

to pat its flanks; Cyril/Squirrel examined the porch,
tried the tap (rusty, of course); and then, the car now broached,
continued the pilgrimage, as you'd expect, to his
boyhood home which (but how could it have stayed as it was? –

and it's not as if he'd ever wanted to go back
after all, to the years when he was living there, stuck)
had a new name on the mailbox, one he needn't know,
and a subtly altered silhouette. So be it. So

we gathered pine cones from the trees his father planted
(replacing the specimens nature had provided)
and drove uphill to the Daysh house, a shell now, its trees
ragged with lichen and tufted with perching lilies.

Jubilee Booklet, 1989

The 'Where did you live' map proved to be
quite a tax on people's memories,
remembering just who had lived where,
when. I hope you can find your name.
Bear in mind that a lot of the roads
have been realigned, so your house
may not have been where I have it marked.
For instance Robert Darlow's house
was on the other side of the road
to where I have it marked, just before
the cutting, out on the point. The facts
are as accurate as I have been able
to establish. I am only human too.

The Archive

There were the 'Opa tapes' – interviews
recorded on a reel-to-reel machine
by an anthropologist grandson, copied
to cassettes, and painstakingly transcribed
like Hansard, with interjections: 'How long?'
'Six months.' 'Six *months!*' [Horrified laughter].

There were letters, postcards, photographs –
familiar, or surprising us among
his or his father's papers; there was a box
of glass negatives never printed off
in our lifetimes: remote, secret views
of a log-scattered landscape under snow;

of a boy in long shorts on a horse;
of a harassed Alice, looking plain for once,
clutching at a huddle of under-fives,
with Eva and that same pleasant-faced boy.
There were receipts and firearms licences;
and there was a line called Trespass, not to be crossed.

State Highway 31

The owners of the land round here
haven't spent their time preserving
obsolete structures for potential
grandfather-chasers to post on Facebook.

They don't prop up decaying trees
with splints and crutches like the King's oak
or some contorted trunk proclaiming
where the early settlers landed.

But what did we expect? After all,
we'd viewed the naked course of the road
on Google Earth, and compared it with
the busy splatter of habitations

on the old sketch map. And at least
we've identified the hillock
where the school stood, then and in its
posthumous life as a hay shed.

As for that iconic row of stumps
in front of – yes – the former homestead,
what apter portrait could we ask
of posterity's heartlessness?

So this is the last time I'll say
how, as we sailed past non-stop
on the way back from Kawhia,
my stomach yearned for just one more glimpse.

NOTES

The Pioneer (13)

The results of the ballot were announced in the *New Zealand Herald* on 27 August 1915 as follows: 'A ballot was held yesterday for six sections of second-class land... there were 120 applications.' Seven people had applied for the section described as Pirongia Survey District. Block IX, Section 17, 150a [acres].

District News (17, 31, 65)

Extracts with this title are from files of the *Waipa Post*, seen in the Alexander Turnbull Library, Wellington. I am also grateful to Catherine Jehly of the Te Awamutu Museum for providing further extracts from this newspaper.

Migrants (22)

Mary Adcock (1825-99), and her second husband Thomas Hardy, with one son each from their first marriages, travelled from Leicester to Utah in 1862. (Mormon websites are very informative.) Buffalo chips were bison dung.

The School (29)

The Moebius strip. As my father showed me when I was nine, cutting along the centre of the double-length loop gives you two separate loops, one looped through the other. It was hard to believe.

Evenings with Mother (47)

The title Cyril has in mind is *The Master of the Shell*, by Talbot Baines Reed (1852-93), first published in book form by the Religious Tract Society, 1901.

The Way Forward (57)

T.U. Wells ran the predecessor to the New Zealand Correspondence School.

Shorthand (61)

Cyril's advertisements were inserted in the *Auckland Star* on 21 and 23 June ('three hours') and 10 December 1920 ('...three days. Short, inexpensive, easy correspondence course.'); there was another in the *New Zealand Herald* on 12 July.

The Bible Student (62)

I should like to tell this clever young man, with his contempt for the Authorised Version, that his distinguished ancestor Dr Robert Tighe (of whom he never heard in his lifetime) was one of the translators appointed by King James. On the other hand his enthusiasm for Charles Taze Russell, whose studies gave rise to the Jehovah's Witnesses, was misplaced – as he very soon realised. All the time I knew him Cyril was an agnostic, but with an energetic devotion to idealistic causes and a perhaps reluctant admiration for an occasional good preacher.

The Sensational (71)

See *The Journal of the Polynesian Society*, vol. 28, no. 110, 1919: 'Rangi-hua-moa', by George Graham, p.107-10, for the origin of the name Te Rau-a-moa. (Modern maps and other sources tend to use the spelling Te Rauamoa, but I have not attempted to be consistent in my usage.)

The Kea Gun (72)

I am indebted to *Papers Past*, on the NZ National Library website, for extracts from newspapers which provided much of the detail here.

Walking Off (83)

Susan Dassler (1887-1988), wife of Oscar and mother of Grace and seven other children, wrote verses and articles for magazines which were collected in 1983 as *From a Pioneer's Pen*.

The Roads Again (84)

In *Days That Have Been* (1966), the prolific author Mary Scott (1888-1979) described her early married life as a farmer's wife a few miles further up Mount Pirongia from the Adcocks.

Jubilee Booklet, 1989 (90)

The words are from John Cleland's 'Editorial' introducing his booklet compiled for the 1989 Ngutunui School 75th Jubilee, which celebrated also Te Rau-a-moa School, 1897-1962.

FSC
www.fsc.org

MIX
Paper from
responsible sources
FSC® C007785